THE ROSARY WITH
FRA ANGELICO AND GIOTTO

The Rosary with

Fra Angelico and Giotto

DOMENICO MARCUCCI

TRANSLATED AND EDITED BY EDMUND C. LANE, SSP

LUMINOUS MYSTERIES COMPILED BY GARY T. JOHNSON

ST PAULS

Alba
House

Scripture passages from The New Testament: St. Paul Catholic
Edition (ST PAULS / Alba House, 2000)

Illustrations for the Joyful, Sorrowful and Glorious Mysteries by Fra Angelico (1387-1455),
Museo di San Marco, Florence, Italy. Copyright Foto Scala, Vigilino, Italy.

Illustrations for the Luminous Mysteries:
Baptism of Christ by Giotto di Bondone (1266-1336), Scrovegni Chapel, Padua, Italy.
Copyright Alinari / Art Resource, NY.
The Wedding at Cana by Giotto di Bondone (1266-1336), Scrovegni Chapel, Padua, Italy.
Copyright Cameraphoto Arte, Venice / Art Resource, NY.
The Resurrection of Lazarus by Giotto di Bondone (1266-1336). Scrovegni Chapel,
Padua, Italy. Copyright Cameraphoto Arte, Venice / Art Resource, NY.
Transfiguration Fresco by Fra Angelico (1387-1455), Museo di San Marco, Florence,
Italy. Copyright Scala / Art Resource, NY.
The Last Supper by Giotto di Bondone (1266-1336). Scrovegni Chapel, Padua, Italy.
Copyright Alinari / Art Resource, NY.

Produced and designed in the United States of America by the
Fathers and Brothers of the Society of St. Paul,
2187 Victory Boulevard, Staten Island, New York 10314-6603,
as part of their communications apostolate.
Printed in Singapore

ISBN: 0-8189-0974-9

Printing Information:

Current Printing - first digit 1 2 3 4 5 6 7 8 9 10

Year of Current Printing - first year shown

2005 2006 2007 2008 2009 2010 2011 2012 2013 2014

Foreword

How the Rosary Came Into Being

The Rosary as we know it hails from the High Middle Ages where it came into being in various medieval monasteries as a substitute for the recitation of the Divine Office on the part of those lay monks and devout lay persons who didn't know how to read. Instead of the 150 psalms, these would recite 150 *Our Fathers* which they counted off on a ring of beads which came to be called by various names in different places: a "crown" of beads or "corona" being the most common appellation.

With the growth in popularity of Marian devotion, which reached its peak in the twelfth century, and with the widespread use of the *Hail Mary* — originally a liturgical antiphon for the Fourth Sunday of Advent made up of just the first part of the prayer — the "Psalter of the Blessed Virgin" composed of 150 *Hail Marys* came into being alongside the "Psalter of the Father." Its diffusion was such that, for all practical purposes, in a very short time it completely supplanted the latter.

It's important to note that the origin of the Rosary was closely related to the Liturgy and, placed in the hands of the unlettered, made it possible for the average person to participate in the prayers recited by the monks in the choir. The universal popularity of this "Marian Psalter" encouraged many to enrich it, building on its original simple repetitive structure. This began with a young German by the name of Henry Kalkar (1328-

1408) who subdivided the 150 *Hail Marys* into 15 decades, separated by recitation of one *Our Father*. A confrere of his, Dominic of Prussia, sometime prior to 1410, proposed a Rosary made up of 50 *Hail Marys* in which to each *Hail Mary*, after the name of Jesus — with which the original prayer ended — a phrase or clause which referred to an episode in the life of Jesus or of the Blessed Virgin would be added: 14 treating the hidden life, 6 referring to the public life, 24 dealing with the passion of Jesus and 6 covering the episodes following His resurrection. Thus the triple division of the mysteries of the Rosary into the *Joyful,* the *Sorrowful* and the *Glorious* was born.

This proposal of Dominic of Prussia met with almost immediate success and during the 1400's assisted in an extraordinary flowering of the Rosary. The mysteries eventually numbered as many as 300 and embraced the entire history of salvation, beginning with creation.

The Work of the Dominicans

The one who contributed more than any other to the launching of the Rosary and who conferred on it that structure with which it has come down to us today was the Dominican friar Alanus de Rupe (1428-1478). His work took place on several levels. First of all, he reformed the prayers, giving the greatest importance to the meditative element, which he called "the soul of the Rosary," rather than to the vocal part which constituted "the body." He divided the episodes in the history of salvation into three sets of fifty, the Joyful, the Sorrowful and the Glorious Mysteries, each of which was further subdivided into five decades corresponding to our present-day fifteen decades, to which Pope John Paul II added five more — the Luminous Mysteries, or the Mysteries of Light — on October 16, 2002.

Alanus de Rupe "ennobled" the whole by attributing the origin of the "Psalter of the Blessed Virgin" to St. Dominic — something that is historically unsubstantiated — and thus spurred his confreres on to make their own the apostolate of the Rosary. The Dominicans have, in fact, since then always propagated its recitation with notable results.

But Friar Alanus was above all an apostle, an outstanding preacher of popular missions, especially in the region of the Netherlands and northern Germany. During these missions he was tireless in his efforts at organizing Confraternities of the Rosary, presenting this prayer as a sure means to grow in the faith and as a powerful weapon against the enemies of the Church.

This last conviction was of extreme importance, so much so that it is spoken of in the first of the papal bulls on the Rosary to come down to us (*Ea quae,* of Sixtus IV, dated May 12, 1479). In it the Rosary is presented as "a pious and devout way of praying, which consists of reciting the angel's salutation every day — in honor of God and of the Blessed Virgin Mary, and against the dangers which threaten the world — as many times as there are Psalms in the Psalter of David." Moreover we cannot overlook how often these Confraternities of the Rosary validly resisted the inroads of Protestantism, so much so that this prayer has almost become a symbol of the Catholic faith.

Finally, this conviction was in a certain way historically confirmed in the victory of Lepanto (October 7, 1571), which Pope St. Pius V attributed more to the "arms" of the Rosary than to the power of the cannons and the valor of the soldiers who fought there. He even went so far as to establish October 7th, the day of the victory, as the day on which the Feast of the Most

Holy Rosary would be celebrated throughout the universal Church.

The definitive structure of the Rosary, which then became codified in the bull *Consueverunt Romani Pontifices,* was given by Albert di Castello, likewise a Dominican friar. He refined this pious practice even further, by suggesting material to be added between each *Hail Mary* as a simple aid to meditation.

During the period of the Renaissance, there were several forms of the Rosary in use far and wide by various religious congregations. Among these the "Rosary of the Seven Sorrows of Mary" recommended by the Servites enjoyed a certain favor. The form which ultimately prevailed, however, was that promoted by the Dominican Order and hailed by a large number of papal documents beginning with the cited *Consueverunt Romani Pontifices* of Pope St. Pius V. The Rosary is presented by it as "the veneration of the Blessed Virgin through the repetition of the angelic salutation 150 times, according to the number of the Psalms of David, interrupting each decade with an *Our Father* and some specific meditations which illustrate the whole life of Our Lord Jesus Christ." Regarding the fruits of the Rosary, the bull was most eloquent indeed: "The faithful who fervently took this prayer to heart, inflamed by its meditations, were transformed into other persons; the darkness of heresy retreated and the light of the Catholic faith made strides once again."

The Rosary and the Life of a Christian

Down through the centuries this prayer, so apparently simple and disarming, has become the focal point of a whole series of values that are symbols, not only of Marian devotion but also of Catholicism itself. The Rosary is a prayer loved by the poor and the rich alike, the unlettered as well as the wise. It has inspired poets, apostles, saints and martyrs. Many have given their lives for Christ clutching the beads of the Rosary in their hands.

The unforgettable Pope John XXIII, uncompromising in his own fidelity to the daily recitation of the Rosary, described in a discourse on May 8, 1963 the milieu created by the common recitation of this prayer around the family hearth: "A poetic atmosphere which places before our eyes the sweet figure of the Madonna is created, the mysteries of the life of Our Lord are made familiar to all, and the challenges of Jesus with respect to our life are caused to be intensely felt.... When this prayer is recited in common one begins to absorb something of what will later become the proper direction for his or her own life." This little booklet has as its aim not only to represent the prayers of the Rosary, thus reaffirming their validity, but also to help one to draw close to the spirit of the Rosary, thus recovering something of the creative faith of such a prayer. Hence the text under each artistic representation announces the mystery that is the subject of that decade's meditation. This is anything but new. Indeed, it is a return to the sources, when the Rosary was first proposed as an aid to deepening and living one's faith.

This form of reciting the Rosary is mentioned and implicitly praised in Pope Paul VI's *Marialis Cultus*: "It is to be noted that, for the precise purpose of favoring contemplation and to help the mind correspond to the words being used, it was the practice at one time — and the custom has been kept in several places — to add to the name of Jesus in every *Hail Mary* a phrase which would recall the mystery that had been announced" (n. 46).

The Rosary, then, is far more varied and complex than what it might at first seem and can, therefore, constitute a prayer adapted to the most diverse circumstances and persons: from a "prayer always at hand" according to a very perceptive expression of a Protestant pastor from Germany, Manfred Seitz to a highly efficacious aid to contemplation.

Finally, taking into account that many will be approaching the Rosary as a totally new prayer for them, both in the writing of the text and in the graphic presentation of the mysteries, we tried to be as clear as possible, indicating in some detail exactly how the prayer unfolds.

The Luminous Mysteries

On October 16, 2002, Pope John Paul II wrote an Apostolic Letter entitled *Rosarium Virginis Mariae* in which he proclaimed October 2002 to October 2003 "The Year of the Rosary." In beginning the 25th year of his Pontificate, he wanted in this way to thank the Lord and his Most Holy Mother for the many graces he had received in the course of his life and ministry through the Rosary. At the same time he thought it opportune, in light of the special needs of the people of the Twenty-First Century, to suggest the addition of five new decades to the Rosary to encourage meditation on the public life of Jesus. He called these new decades, the Luminous Mysteries or the Mysteries of Light. The following paragraphs are excerpted from his Letter.

* * *

"The whole mystery of Christ is a mystery of light. He is the 'light of the world' (Jn 8:12). Yet this truth emerges in a special way during the years of his public life, when he proclaims the Gospel of the Kingdom. In proposing to the Christian community five significant moments — 'luminous' mysteries — during this phase of Christ's life, I think that the following can be fittingly singled out: (1) his Baptism in the Jordan, (2) his self-manifestation at the wedding of Cana, (3) his proclamation of the Kingdom of God, with his call to conversion, (4) his Transfiguration, and finally, (5) his institution of the Eucharist, as the sacramental expression of the Paschal Mystery.

"Each of these mysteries is a *revelation of the Kingdom now present in the very person of Jesus.* The Baptism in the Jordan is first of all a mystery of light. Here, as Christ descends into the waters, the innocent one who became 'sin' for our sake (cf. 2 Cor 5:21), the heavens open wide and the voice of the Father declares him the beloved Son (cf. Mt 3:17 and parallels), while the Spirit descends on him to invest him with the mission which he is to carry out. Another mystery of light is the first of the signs, given at Cana (cf. Jn 2:1-12), when Christ changes water into wine and opens the hearts of the disciples to faith, thanks to the intervention of Mary, the first among believers. Another mystery of light is the preaching by which Jesus proclaims the coming of the Kingdom of God, calls to conversion (cf. Mk 1:15) and forgives the sins of all who draw near to him in humble trust (cf. Mk 2:3-13; Lk 7:47-48): the inauguration of that ministry of mercy which he continues to exercise until the end of the world, particularly through the Sacrament of Reconciliation which he has entrusted to his Church (cf. Jn 20:22-23). The mystery of light *par excellence* is the Transfiguration, traditionally believed to have taken place on Mount Tabor. The glory of the Godhead shines forth from the face of Christ as the Father commands the astonished Apostles to 'listen to him' (cf. Lk 9:35 and parallels) and to prepare to experience with him the agony of the Passion, so as to come with him to the joy of the Resurrection and a life transfigured by the Holy Spirit. A final mystery of light is the institution of the Eucharist, in which Christ offers his body and blood as food under the signs of bread and wine, and testifies 'to the end' his love for humanity (Jn 13:1), for whose salvation he will offer himself in sacrifice.

"In these mysteries, apart from the miracle at Cana, *the presence of Mary remains in the background.* The Gospels make only the briefest reference to her occasional presence at one moment or other during the preaching of Jesus (cf. Mk 3:31-5; Jn 2:12), and they give no indication that she was present at the Last Supper and the institution of the Eucharist. Yet the role she assumed at Cana in some way accompanies Christ throughout his ministry. The revelation made directly by the Father at the Baptism in the Jordan and echoed by John the Baptist is placed upon Mary's lips at Cana, and it becomes the great maternal counsel which Mary addresses to the Church of every age: 'Do whatever he tells you' (Jn 2:5). This counsel is a fitting introduction to the words and signs of Christ's public ministry and it forms the Marian foundation of all the 'mysteries of light'."

Fra Angelico's "Armadio degli Argenti"

The illustrations of the Joyful, Sorrowful and Glorious Mysteries of the Rosary that appear in this little booklet are by Fra Angelico (Guido di Pietro) who was born in Vicchio nel Mugello around 1400 (some texts indicate a date as early as

1387) and died in Rome in 1455. Almost all of these have been taken from one work, the so-called *Armadio degli Argenti* ("The Silver Closet") presently preserved in the Museum of San Marco in Florence. The three exceptions in this booklet are the paintings of *Mary's Visit to Elizabeth, The Transfiguration,* and *The Dormition* which are reproductions of other works by the same artist.

"The Silver Closet" was commissioned by Piero de Medici, the sickly brother of Lorenzo the Magnificent, around the year 1448 and was probably painted some years later, around 1450. Originally the 35 little paintings of which the whole work was made up decorated the panels of the doors to a huge closet destined for the conservation of the most precious silver votive offerings to the church of the Annunciation, the most popular Marian sanctuary in Florence. By 1461 the work had already suffered some abuse and another 6 pictures were added to it. In 1782 the whole closet disappeared and the doors were dismantled. Fortunately the paintings of Fra Angelico were saved, but critics have never succeeded in establishing the original order in which they were executed.

"The Silver Closet" is the last important work of this great painter. In a way it is his testament as both an artist and a "preacher." The 35 little paintings — each measuring approximately 15" by 14" — embrace the completion of the "History of Salvation" understood as the fulfillment of the promises made in the Old Testament. The numerous inscriptions with which the work is strewn, containing biblical texts, complete and explain the various representations. These, in their turn, are framed between two symbolic figures which constitute the key to their interpretation: the "Mystical Wheel" at the beginning and the "Law of Love" at the end. The "Mystical Wheel" which takes

13

its inspiration from the celebrated vision of Ezekiel (chapter 1) represents the rapport between the Old and the New Testaments: the New is contained in the Old and complements it. In its turn, the panel of the "Law of Love," at the end of the work presents love as the ultimate meaning of all the Law.

Even in "The Silver Closet," and perhaps in a more complete way than in his other works, we find realized that wonderful formal synthesis which is characteristic of Fra Angelico and which never ceases to amaze the critics: he was the perfect Renaissance painter, a consummate technician with a refined knowledge of anatomy and perspective. And still he manages to render in a very simple and immediate way a sense of the sacred where his contemporaries sacrificed it for the sake of being faithful to the human. Fra Angelico, in order to represent the sacred, in this work perhaps less than in those which preceded it, doesn't need to stylize the figures or heap upon them a lot of halos or place them in a scene with golden backgrounds. Brilliant colors in a composition that is both recollected and lacking in elements capable of distracting, into which he placed figures who were at one and the same time intense and composed, were enough for him.

All these characteristics make these illustrations of the monk who painted them ideal for accompanying and perhaps even inspiring our contemplation of the mysteries of the Rosary.

Many persons like to begin the recitation of the Rosary with the sign of the cross and the prayer:

V. O God, come to my assistance.
R. O Lord, make haste to help me.

Glory be to the Father, and to the Son and to the Holy Spirit, as it was in the beginning, is now, and ever shall be world without end. Amen.

After the *Glory be* it has become customary in many places to recite this prayer, which traces its origin to the apparitions at Fatima (May - October, 1917):

O my Jesus, forgive us our sins, save us from the fires of hell. Take all souls to heaven, especially those who have most need of your mercy.

Taking the crucifix of the Rosary in hand, the Creed is then recited:

I believe in God, the Father almighty,
Creator of heaven and earth;
And in Jesus Christ, His only Son, our Lord;
Who was conceived by the Holy Spirit,
Born of the Virgin Mary,
Suffered under Pontius Pilate,
Was crucified, died and was buried;
He descended into hell;
The third day, He rose again from the dead;

He ascended into heaven and sits at the right hand
of God, the Father almighty;
From whence He shall come to judge
the living and the dead.
I believe in the Holy Spirit;
The holy Catholic Church;
The communion of saints;
The forgiveness of sins;
The resurrection of the body;
And life everlasting. Amen.

The five beads that follow can be used to recite an *Our Father,* three *Hail Marys* to obtain the three theological gifts of faith, hope and charity, and a *Glory be.* The mystery of the first decade is then announced, using the traditional text as found beneath each illustration. This may be followed by a reading of the biblical citation and the enunciation of the intentions for which the decade is being offered. When only one Rosary is being recited during the day, then, the Holy Father suggests in his Apostolic Letter *Rosarium Virginis Mariae*, on Mondays and Saturdays it would be appropriate to recite the *Joyful Mysteries*; on Tuesdays and Fridays, the *Sorrowful Mysteries*; on Wednesdays and Sundays, the *Glorious Mysteries*; and on Thursdays, the *Luminous Mysteries*. Each decade begins with an *Our Father,* followed by 10 *Hail Marys,* a *Glory be,* and the prayer, *O my Jesus.*

The five beads at the end of the Rosary leading back to the crucifix are sometimes used for the recitation of a *Hail Holy Queen,* and *Our Father, Hail Mary,* and *Glory be* for the intentions of the Holy Father, followed by an *Act of Contrition*:

O my God, I am heartily sorry
  for having offended You.
I detest all my sins
  because of Your just punishments,
  but most of all
  because they offend You, my God,
  Who are all good and deserving of all my love.
I firmly resolve, with the help of Your grace,
  to sin no more and
  to avoid the near occasions of sin.

For an even more reflective and meditative recitation, everything unfolds as above except that, following the name of Jesus in each *Hail Mary,* the corresponding phrase found in this little booklet is added. The second part of the prayer *Holy Mary, Mother of God, pray for us sinners, now and at the hour of our death* is said only after the 10th *Hail Mary* and just before the *Glory be.*

The Annunciation

the Archangel Gabriel declares to the Virgin Mary
that she is about to become the Mother of the Lord.
Mary accepts, declaring herself to be
the "Handmaid of the Lord."

Biblical Citation

The angel Gabriel was sent from God to a town of Galilee called Nazareth to a virgin betrothed to a man named Joseph, of the house of David. And the virgin's name was Mary. The angel said to her, "Do not be afraid, Mary, for you have found favor with God. Behold, you will conceive in your womb and bear a son, and you shall name him Jesus. He will be great and will be called Son of the Most High. The Lord God will give him the throne of David his father, and he will rule over the house of Jacob forever. Of his kingdom there will be no end." Then Mary said, "Behold, I am the handmaid of the Lord. May it be done to me according to your word." (Lk 1:26-27, 30-33, 38)

Prayer Intentions

- That all Christians might present Christ to the world as its Savior.
- For the Jewish people.

Our Father...

Hail Mary, full of grace, the Lord is with you. Blessed are you among women, and blessed is the fruit of your womb, JESUS...

1 ... who has freed us from the sin of Adam.
2 ... for whom the patriarchs and the prophets sighed.
3 ... for whom you and Joseph waited in an attitude of prayer.
4 ... who was sent to us by the Father who loves us.
5 ... who became man out of love.
6 ... whose coming was made known by the message of the angel Gabriel.
7 ... whose announced coming disturbed you at first.
8 ... whom you welcomed in faith.
9 ... who was conceived by the work of the Holy Spirit.
10 ... who was adored by the angels.

Holy Mary, Mother of God, pray for us sinners, now and at the hour of our death. Amen.

Glory be... O my Jesus...

Mary Visits Her Cousin Elizabeth

*M*ary sets out to visit St. Elizabeth who was carrying
St. John the Baptist in her womb. At Mary's greeting,
the baby leaped with joy and Elizabeth gave praise to
God for the wonderful work He was accomplishing in Mary.

Biblical Citation

As soon as Elizabeth heard Mary's greeting, the infant leaped in her womb. And she, filled with the Holy Spirit, cried out in a loud voice, saying, "Blessed are you among women, and blessed is the fruit of your womb! Who am I that the mother of my Lord should come to me? At the moment the sound of your greeting reached my ears, the infant in my womb leaped for joy. Blessed are you because you believed that the word spoken to you by the Lord would be fulfilled." And Mary said, "My soul proclaims the greatness of the Lord; my spirit finds its joy in God my savior!" (Lk 1:41-47)

Prayer Intentions

- For all expectant mothers.
- For missionaries everywhere.

Our Father…

Hail Mary, full of grace, the Lord is with you. Blessed are you among women, and blessed is the fruit of your womb, JESUS…

1. … who dwelt for nine months in your womb.
2. … who upon entering this world, offered himself to the Father.
3. … who filled you with joy by his presence.
4. … whose conception caused Joseph some needless concern.
5. … who is the Savior of all the elect.
6. … who inspired you to visit Elizabeth.
7. … who caused John the Baptist to leap for joy at your salutation.
8. … whom you acknowledged as the Savior in the Magnificat.
9. … who made you solicitous for the welfare of your cousin Elizabeth.
10. … who was one with you.

Holy Mary, Mother of God, pray for us sinners, now and at the hour of our death. Amen.

Glory be… O my Jesus…

The Birth of Jesus

Jesus was born in a grotto in Bethlehem
amid the most squalid poverty because no one would
take Joseph and Mary in.

Biblical Citation

While they were there, the time for Mary's deliverance arrived and she gave birth to her firstborn son whom she wrapped in swaddling clothes and laid in a manger because there was no room for them in the inn. Now there were shepherds in the district who were living in the fields, keeping watch over their flocks by night. The angel of the Lord appeared to them and the glory of the Lord shone around them. The shepherds were overcome with fear. But the angel said to them, "Fear not, for behold, I bring tidings of great joy for all the people. Today, in the city of David, a savior has been born for you who is both Messiah and Lord." (Lk 2:6-11)

Prayer Intentions

- That families might be open to the gift of new life.
- For all those who are in need.

Our Father...

Hail Mary, full of grace, the Lord is with you. Blessed are you among women, and blessed is the fruit of your womb, JESUS...

1 ... who was not welcomed by the inhabitants of Bethlehem.
2 ... who was born in a stable.
3 ... to whom you gave birth with immense love in your heart.
4 ... to whom you consecrated your virginity.
5 ... whose birth was made easier by the song of the angels.
6 ... who was the most handsome of the sons of men.
7 ... who was visited by the shepherds.
8 ... who was circumcised according to the prescriptions of the Law.
9 ... whose name means "God Saves."
10 ... who was adored by the Magi.

Holy Mary, Mother of God, pray for us sinners, now and at the hour of our death. Amen.

Glory be... O my Jesus...

The Presentation of Jesus in the Temple

*M*ary and Joseph, faithful to the Law of Moses, present the baby Jesus in the Temple and fulfill that which was prescribed for their purification.

Biblical Citation

When the time came for their purification according to the Law of Moses, they took the child to Jerusalem to present him to the Lord. Simeon, a just man, moved by the Spirit, came that day to the Temple. And when the parents brought in the child Jesus to perform the customary practices of the Law, he took him in his arms and blessed God. Then he said to Mary, his mother, "This child is destined for the fall and rise of many in Israel, for he is to be a sign of contradiction so that the thoughts of many hearts may be laid bare. And a sword will pierce your soul as well." (Lk 2:22, 25, 27-28, 34-35)

Prayer Intentions

- For the Christian initiation of youth.
- For the Jewish people.

Our Father...

Hail Mary, full of grace, the Lord is with you. Blessed are you among women, and blessed is the fruit of your womb, JESUS...

1 ... who was obedient to the Law like you.
2 ... who as the firstborn of the Father was consecrated to the Lord.
3 ... for love of whom you submitted to the Law of purification.
4 ... who was welcomed by Simeon and Anna with hymns of joy.
5 ... who was redeemed by the offering of two turtle doves.
6 ... whom Herod sought to kill in the Slaughter of the Innocents.
7 ... who fled with you and Joseph into Egypt.
8 ... who was an immigrant in a foreign land.
9 ... who returned with you to Nazareth.
10 ... who grew in wisdom, age and grace before both God and men.

Holy Mary, Mother of God, pray for us sinners, now and at the hour of our death. Amen.

Glory be... O my Jesus...

The Finding of Jesus in the Temple

the child Jesus remained three days
in the Temple in Jerusalem, unknown to Joseph and Mary,
to witness to them that he had come into the world
to do the will of his heavenly Father.

Biblical Citation

After they had completed the three days of the feast, and were returning home, the boy Jesus remained behind in Jerusalem without his parents' knowing it. After three days they found him in the Temple, seated in the midst of the teachers, listening to them and asking them questions. On seeing him, they were astonished, and his mother said to him, "Son, why have you done this to us? Your father and I have been looking for you anxiously." To which he replied, "But why were you looking for me? Did you not know that I had to be in my Father's house?" (Lk 2:43, 46, 48-49)

Prayer Intentions

- For vocations.
- For understanding between parents and their children.

Our Father...

Hail Mary, full of grace, the Lord is with you. Blessed are you among women, and blessed is the fruit of your womb, JESUS...

1 ... who lived a life of hard work at Nazareth.
2 ... who was found in the Temple among the teachers.
3 ... who was baptized by John in the Jordan.
4 ... who was tempted by Satan in the desert.
5 ... who went about preaching the reign of God.
6 ... who healed the sick, cast out demons and raised the dead.
7 ... who chose the twelve apostles.
8 ... who was transfigured on the Mount.
9 ... who washed the feet of the apostles.
10 ... who instituted the Eucharist.

Holy Mary, Mother of God, pray for us sinners, now and at the hour of our death. Amen.

Glory be... O my Jesus...

His Baptism in the Jordan

Jesus humbly consents to be baptized by John the Baptist
in the waters of the Jordan River, investing him
with the mission that he is to carry out and
revealing the mystery of the Trinity.

Biblical Citation

At that time Jesus came from Galilee to be baptized by John at the Jordan. John tried to prevent him and said, "*I* need to be baptized by *you*, and you are coming to me?" But in answer Jesus said to him, "Let it be, for now — it is fitting for us to fulfill all God's will in this way." Then he let him. After he was baptized Jesus at once came up from the water and, behold, the heavens were opened and he saw the Spirit of God descending upon him like a dove. And, behold a voice from Heaven said, "This is My Beloved Son in whom I am well pleased." (Mt 3:13-17)

Prayer Intentions

- For peace.
- For missionaries everywhere.

Our Father...

Hail Mary, full of grace, the Lord is with you. Blessed are you among women, and blessed is the fruit of your womb, JESUS...

1 ... who came from Galilee to John at the Jordan, to be baptized by him.
2 ... whom John the Baptist called "The Lamb of God, who takes away the sin of the world."
3 ... who overcame John's reluctance by humbly fulfilling everything laid down by God.
4 ... who descended into the waters.
5 ... for whom the heavens opened up wide.
6 ... whom the Father declared to be His Beloved Son.
7 ... on whom the Spirit descended like a dove and remained on him.
8 ... whose baptism prepares us to receive the Messiah according to God's plan.
9 ... who made us truly members of the Lord's body.
10 ... who baptizes, not with water, but with the Holy Spirit.

Holy Mary, Mother of God, pray for us sinners, now and at the hour of our death. Amen.

Glory be... O my Jesus...

His Self-Manifestation
at the Wedding Feast of Cana

the first of the signs took place at Cana when Christ
changed water into wine and opened the hearts
of the disciples to faith, thanks to the intervention
of Mary, the first among believers.

Biblical Citation

On the third day there was a wedding in Cana of Galilee, and Jesus' mother was there. Now Jesus and his disciples had also been invited. When the wine ran out Jesus' mother said to him, "They have no wine." Jesus replied, "What do you want from me, woman? My hour hasn't come yet." His mother said to the servants, "Do whatever he tells you." Jesus said to them, "Fill the water jars with water." And they filled them to the brim. When the head steward tasted the water which had become wine, he called the bridegroom and said to him, "Every man first puts out the good wine, then when they're drunk he puts out the lesser wine; *you've* kept the good wine till *now*!" Jesus did this, the first of his signs, at Cana in Galilee and revealed his glory and his disciples believed in him. (Jn 2:1-5, 7, 9-11)

Prayer Intentions

- For the family.
- For those who serve God in their workplaces.

Our Father…

Hail Mary, full of grace, the Lord is with you. Blessed are you among women, and blessed is the fruit of your womb, JESUS…

1 … whose presence blesses love between man and woman, joined in marriage.
2 … of whom you were the first among believers.
3 … to whom you pointed out your concern.
4 … who heeded your intercession.
5 … of whom, you said: "Do whatever he tells you."
6 … whose words the servants obeyed precisely.
7 … who was the good wine, held back until the right time.
8 … whose gift was generous, filled to the brim.
9 … who opens our hearts to faith.
10 … whose signs reveal his glory.

Holy Mary, Mother of God, pray for us sinners, now and at the hour of our death. Amen.

Glory be… O my Jesus…

His Proclamation of the Kingdom of God, with His Calls to Conversion

by his preaching and miracles Jesus proclaims the Kingdom
of God, calls to conversion, and forgives the sins
of all who draw near to him in humble trust.

Biblical Citation

Martha said to Jesus, "Lord, if you'd been here my brother would not have died." Jesus said to her, "Your brother will rise!" Martha said to him, "I know that he will rise at the resurrection on the last day." Jesus said to her, "I am the resurrection and the life! Whoever believes in me, even if he should die, will live, and everyone who lives and believes in me shall never die." (Jn 11:21-26)

"Blessed are the poor in spirit, for theirs is the Kingdom of Heaven." (Mt 5:3)

"The appointed time has come and the Kingdom of God is at hand; repent and believe in the good news!" (Mk 1:14-15)

Prayer Intentions

- For the sick and for caregivers.
- For the conversion of sinners and the reevangelization of the faith in historically Christian areas.

Our Father...

Hail Mary, full of grace, the Lord is with you. Blessed are you among women, and blessed is the fruit of your womb, JESUS...

1 ... who called the Apostles, making them fishers of men.
2 ... who taught as one with authority, and not as the scribes.
3 ... who healed the sick, restored sight to the blind and forgave sinners.
4 ... who proclaimed the Kingdom of God.
5 ... who showed a special love for the poor and needy.
6 ... to whom the crowds came in faith, seeking healing.
7 ... who blesses those who have not seen, and yet believe.
8 ... who called blessed the peacemakers and those persecuted for his sake.
9 ... who calls us to make disciples of all nations.
10 ... who will be with us always, to the end of the age.

Holy Mary, Mother of God, pray for us sinners, now and at the hour of our death. Amen.

Glory be... O my Jesus...

His Transfiguration

Jesus takes three of his disciples with him to the top of a high mountain and he is transfigured before them, preparing them to experience the agony of the Passion and giving them a foretaste of the joy of his glorious Resurrection.

Biblical Citation

He took Peter, John, and James and went up the mountain to pray. And it happened that while he was praying the appearance of his face was altered, and his clothing became a dazzling white. And, behold, two men were speaking with him, Moses and Elijah, who were seen in glory speaking about his Exodus, which he would bring to completion in Jerusalem. Peter as well as those with him had been overcome by sleep, but when they were fully awake they saw his glory and the two men standing with him. A cloud arose and overshadowed them, and a voice came from the cloud, saying, "This is My Son, My Chosen; hear him!" (Lk 9:28-32, 34-35)

Prayer Intentions

- That we may be prepared for our own suffering and tribulation.
- That we may see God face-to-face in glory.

Our Father…

Hail Mary, full of grace, the Lord is with you. Blessed are you among women, and blessed is the fruit of your womb, JESUS…

1 … who led Peter, James and John up a high mountain apart.
2 … whose face shone like the sun and whose garments became white as light.
3 … with whom Moses and Elijah were talking.
4 … who was overshadowed by a cloud.
5 … of whom the Father said: "This is My Son, My Chosen; hear him!"
6 … before whom the disciples fell on their knees, filled with awe.
7 … who touched his disciples, saying, "Rise, and have no fear."
8 … who spoke of his Passion, Death and Resurrection.
9 … who is endowed with glory and majesty in Heaven.
10 … who gives power to become children of God to all who believe in his name.

Holy Mary, Mother of God, pray for us sinners, now and at the hour of our death. Amen.

Glory be… O my Jesus…

His Institution of the Eucharist, the Sacramental Reenactment of the Paschal Mystery

Christ institutes the Eucharist on the night when he was
betrayed, offering his body and blood as food
under the signs of bread and wine, commanding us
to do this in remembrance of him.

Biblical Citation

When the hour came he sat down at table with the apostles. And he said to them, "With what longing have I longed to eat this Passover with you before I suffer, for I tell you that I will not eat it again until it is fulfilled in the Kingdom of God." Then he took a cup, blessed it, and said, "Take this and divide it among yourselves, for I tell you I will not drink the fruit of the vine from this moment until the Kingdom of God comes." Then he took bread, blessed it, broke it, and gave it to them, saying, "This is my body which is given up for you — do this in my remembrance." Likewise he took the cup after they had eaten and said, "This cup is the new covenant in my blood which is poured out for you." (Lk 22:14-20)

Prayer Intentions

- For a greater love and appreciation of the real presence of Christ in the Eucharist.
- For holy vocations to the priesthood and religious life.

Our Father...

Hail Mary, full of grace, the Lord is with you. Blessed are you among women, and blessed is the fruit of your womb, JESUS...

1 ... who knew that his hour had come to go to the Father.
2 ... who gave thanks to God on the night before he died.
3 ... who instituted the Eucharist for the nourishment of our souls.
4 ... who offered his body for us and inaugurated the new covenant in his blood.
5 ... who told us to "Do this in remembrance of me."
6 ... whose death we proclaim until he comes as often as we eat this bread and drink this wine.
7 ... who offered himself in sacrifice for our salvation.
8 ... who offers consolation and strength to us in the Eucharist.
9 ... who loved his disciples in the world to the end.
10 ... who remains with us always in the Blessed Sacrament.

Holy Mary, Mother of God, pray for us sinners, now and at the hour of our death. Amen.

Glory be... O my Jesus...

The Agony in the Garden of Gethsemane

Just before his passion, Jesus prayed that the reality of the suffering and death which awaited him might be taken away, but he nonetheless willed to perfectly fulfill whatever it was that the Father wanted him to do.

Biblical Citation

Going out, he went as usual to the Mount of Olives where his disciples followed him. Arriving at the place, he said to them, "Pray that you may not succumb to temptation." Then, withdrawing from them a stone's throw away, he knelt down to pray, saying, "Father, if you will, take this cup from me; nonetheless, not my will but yours be done." Then, to comfort him, an angel from heaven appeared to him. He was in such anguish that he prayed all the more intensely. And his sweat became as drops of blood which fell upon the ground. (Lk 22:39-44)

Prayer Intentions

- For those persecuted for the sake of the Gospel.
- For those who are unable to comprehend or accept their suffering.

Our Father...

Hail Mary, full of grace, the Lord is with you. Blessed are you among women, and blessed is the fruit of your womb, JESUS...

1 ... who went out to the Mount of Olives, to the Garden of Gethsemane.
2 ... who addressed his Father in insistent prayer.
3.... who was left alone by the apostles.
4 ... who suffered mortal anguish in the Garden.
5 ... who sweat blood.
6 ... who was consoled by an angel.
7 ... who embraced the will of his heavenly Father.
8 ... who courageously confronted his adversaries in the Garden.
9 ... who was betrayed by Judas.
10 ... who was abandoned by all his friends.

Holy Mary, Mother of God, pray for us sinners, now and at the hour of our death. Amen.

Glory be... O my Jesus...

The Scourging at the Pillar

Consigned to a pagan tribunal,
Jesus underwent a cruel and bloody scourging.

Biblical Citation

"Which one do you want me to release to you, Barabbas or Jesus, who is called the Messiah?" The chief priests and the elders persuaded the crowd to ask for Barabbas and to have Jesus put to death. So the governor repeated the question, "Which of the two do you want me to release to you?" They answered, "Barabbas!" Pilate then asked, "What am I to do then with Jesus who is called the Messiah?" They all cried out, "Crucify him!" So he released Barabbas to them and, after having had Jesus scourged, he handed him over to be crucified. (Mt 27:17, 20-22, 26)

Prayer Intentions

- For all those who are in prison.
- For greater respect for human life.

Our Father...

Hail Mary, full of grace, the Lord is with you. Blessed are you among women, and blessed is the fruit of your womb, JESUS...

1 ... who was arrested and bound.
2 ... who was struck on the cheek in front of Caiaphas.
3 ... who was denied three times by Peter.
4 ... who was sneered at by Herod.
5 ... who was stripped of his garments.
6 ... who was insulted by the soldiers.
7 ... who was tied to a pillar.
8 ... who was cruelly scourged.
9 ... whose flesh was made an open wound.
10 ... who shed his blood for me.

Holy Mary, Mother of God, pray for us sinners, now and at the hour of our death. Amen.

Glory be... O my Jesus...

The Crowning With Thorns

Left to the mercy of the soldiers, Jesus
was made a laughing-stock and subjected to the most
atrocious jests. A crown of thorns was placed
upon his head and driven into his flesh.

Biblical Citation

Then the soldiers of the governor took Jesus inside the praetorium and gathered the whole cohort around him. After stripping him of his clothes, they threw a scarlet military cloak around his shoulders. Then, weaving a crown of thorns, they placed it on his head, and thrust a reed in his right hand. Kneeling before him, they mocked him, saying, "Hail, King of the Jews!" Then spitting on him, they took the reed and kept striking him on the head. (Mt 27:27-30)

Prayer Intentions

- For those who are persecuted for the faith.
- For the military.

Our Father…

Hail Mary, full of grace, the Lord is with you. Blessed are you among women, and blessed is the fruit of your womb, JESUS…

1 … who suffered for us sinners.
2 … who had his eyes covered with a blindfold.
3 … who was spat upon in the face.
4 … who was dressed in a scarlet cloak.
5 … who had a reed placed in his hand like a scepter.
6 … who was crowned with thorns.
7 … who was mocked as a king.
8 … who was outrageously abused and insulted.
9 … whose head and face streamed with blood.
10 … whose kingdom is not of this world.

Holy Mary, Mother of God, pray for us sinners, now and at the hour of our death. Amen.

Glory be… O my Jesus…

Jesus Carries His Cross to Calvary

Condemned to death by Pilate, Jesus is forced
to carry on his shoulders the heavy weight of the cross
on which he was to die on Calvary.

Biblical Citation

After they had mocked him, they stripped him of the cloak, dressed him in his own clothes and led him off to be crucified. Along the road they encountered a Cyrenian by the name of Simon and they forced him to take up the cross behind Jesus. (Mt 27:31-32)

Prayer Intentions

- For those who are scandalized by the cross.
- For judges and magistrates.

Our Father...

Hail Mary, full of grace, the Lord is with you. Blessed are you among women, and blessed is the fruit of your womb, JESUS...

1 ... who was presented before the mob with the words, "Behold the man!"
2 ... whom the people rejected in favor of Barabbas.
3 ... who was unjustly accused by false witnesses.
4 ... who was condemned to death by Pilate.
5 ... who lovingly took up the cross for our salvation.
6 ... who fell several times under the heavy weight of the cross.
7 ... who was assisted on the way by Simon of Cyrene.
8 ... whom you met on the way to Calvary.
9 ... whose face Veronica wiped with her veil.
10 ... who consoled the weeping women of Jerusalem.

Holy Mary, Mother of God, pray for us sinners, now and at the hour of our death. Amen.

Glory be... O my Jesus...

Jesus Dies on the Cross

Stripped of his clothes and nailed to the cross, Jesus dies amidst the most atrocious agony, forgiving his enemies and surrendering his spirit to his heavenly Father.

Biblical Citation

When Jesus saw his mother and the disciple whom he loved standing there, he said to his mother, "Woman, behold your son!" Then he said to the disciple, "Behold your mother!" (Jn 19:26-27)

Crying out in a loud voice, Jesus said, "Father, into your hands I commend my spirit!" Then, having said this, he died. (Lk 23:46)

Prayer Intentions

- For the dying.
- For those who find themselves unable to forgive.

Our Father…

Hail Mary, full of grace, the Lord is with you. Blessed are you among women, and blessed is the fruit of your womb, JESUS…

1 … who was nailed to a cross.

2 … who was given a mixture of gall and vinegar to drink.

3 … who was crucified between two thieves.

4 … who united you to his own sufferings.

5 … who uttered seven last words from the cross.

6 … who felt he had been abandoned by his Father.

7 … for whom the universe wept.

8 … who died on the cross.

9 … whose heart was pierced by a lance.

10 … who was laid to rest in a sepulcher nearby.

Holy Mary, Mother of God, pray for us sinners, now and at the hour of our death. Amen.

Glory be… O my Jesus…

The Resurrection of Jesus

On the third day, Jesus rose victorious
from the grave and appeared to many of his disciples
over the course of the next forty days.

Biblical Citation

Very early on the first day of the week, the women took the spices which they had prepared and went to the tomb. They found the stone rolled back from the tomb, but upon entering it, they did not find the body of the Lord Jesus. While they were in a state of confusion over this, two men in dazzling garments appeared to them. Terrified, they bowed their heads to the ground. The men said to them, "Why are you looking among the dead for him who is alive? He is not here, but has risen." And so they returned from the tomb and announced all these things to the eleven and all the rest. (Lk 24:1-6, 9)

Prayer Intentions

- That Easter might be ever more at the center of the life of the Church.
- For those who are in mourning.

Our Father...

Hail Mary, full of grace, the Lord is with you. Blessed are you among women, and blessed is the fruit of your womb, JESUS...

1 ... who descended to the abode of the dead.

2 ... who is the savior of the ancient patriarchs.

3 ... who rose from the sepulcher.

4 ... who was victorious over sin and death.

5 ... whose body was glorified in the resurrection.

6 ... to whom all power on earth and in heaven has been given.

7 ... who appeared to you and to the disciples.

8 ... who ate and drank with the apostles.

9 ... who spoke of the reign of God.

10 ... who sent the apostles into the world.

Holy Mary, Mother of God, pray for us sinners, now and at the hour of our death. Amen.

Glory be... O my Jesus...

The Ascension Into Heaven

the risen Lord ascended into heaven
where he sits in glory at the right hand of the Father
awaiting his return at the end of time.

Biblical Citation

Jesus was lifted up before their eyes and a cloud hid him from their sight. While they were standing there looking intently at the sky as he was leaving, suddenly two men dressed in white garments stood beside them and said, "Men of Galilee, why are you standing here gazing at the sky? This Jesus who has been taken up from you into heaven will return one day in the same way as you have seen him going up to heaven." (Ac 1:9-11)

Prayer Intentions

- That every Christian might recognize that they are missionaries.
- For all those who have not yet heard the good news.

Our Father...

Hail Mary, full of grace, the Lord is with you. Blessed are you among women, and blessed is the fruit of your womb, JESUS...

1 ... who promised the Holy Spirit to the apostles.
2 ... who brought the disciples together on the Mount of Olives.
3 ... who blessed his disciples.
4 ... who ascended into heaven.
5 ... who was welcomed by the angels and the blessed in heaven.
6 ... who sits now at the right hand of the Father.
7 ... who has been made judge of the living and the dead.
8 ... who will return one day in power and glory.
9 ... who will reward the good and punish the wicked.
10 ... who has prepared a place for us in his kingdom.

Holy Mary, Mother of God, pray for us sinners, now and at the hour of our death. Amen.

Glory be... O my Jesus...

THIRD GLORIOUS MYSTERY

The Descent of the Holy Spirit

A s Jesus promised, the Holy Spirit descended
upon Mary and the disciples on the Feast of Pentecost,
strengthening and enlightening them.

Biblical Citation

When the days of Pentecost were drawing to a close, they were all together in the same place. All of a sudden there came from the sky a rumbling like that of a strong driving wind, filling the whole house where they were assembled. Tongues as of fire appeared which parted and came to rest on each of them. They were filled with the Holy Spirit and began to express themselves in other tongues as the Holy Spirit enabled them to speak. (Ac 2:1-4)

Prayer Intentions

- For all leaders of the Church.
- For Christian unity.

Our Father...

Hail Mary, full of grace, the Lord is with you. Blessed are you among women, and blessed is the fruit of your womb, JESUS...

1 ... from whom, in union with the Father, the Holy Spirit proceeds.
2 ... who sent the Holy Spirit upon the apostles.
3 ... whose Spirit manifested itself in tongues of fire.
4 ... who gives the Spirit of wisdom in the Scriptures.
5 ... who pours forth the Holy Spirit into our hearts.
6 ... who was guided by the Spirit throughout his life.
7 ... who looks for the fruits of the Spirit in our lives.
8 ... who sends the Holy Spirit and his seven gifts to his Church.
9 ... who wants the Holy Spirit to reign in our hearts.
10 ... who conquers the forces of evil through the Spirit.

Holy Mary, Mother of God, pray for us sinners, now and at the hour of our death. Amen.

Glory be... O my Jesus...

FOURTH GLORIOUS MYSTERY

The Assumption of Mary Into Heaven

When her life came to an end,
Mary was assumed body and soul into heaven
where she reigns in glory with her Son.

Biblical Citation

Then God's sanctuary in heaven was opened, and the ark of his covenant could be seen therein. Then a great sign appeared in the sky, a woman clothed with the sun, with the moon under her feet and a crown of twelve stars on her head. (Rv 11:19; 12:1)

Prayer Intentions

- That all Christians might present Christ to the world as its Savior.
- For the Jewish people.

Our Father...

Hail Mary, full of grace, the Lord is with you. Blessed are you among women, and blessed is the fruit of your womb, JESUS...

1 ... who made you the masterpiece of his creation.
2 ... who filled you with his grace from the first moment of your life.
3 ... who caused the world to rejoice at your birth.
4 ... who inspired your total consecration to God.
5 ... who preserved you from all sin.
6 ... who adorned you with every virtue.
7 ... of whom you were the ever virgin mother.
8 ... who was the author of your alliance with the Trinity.
9 ... who met you at the time of your loving death.
10 ... who raised you up and assumed you into heaven.

Holy Mary, Mother of God, pray for us sinners, now and at the hour of our death. Amen.

Glory be... O my Jesus...

FIFTH GLORIOUS MYSTERY

The Coronation of Mary
as Queen of Heaven

Mary is seated in glory among the angels
and saints of heaven, the queen and first fruits
of our redeemed humanity.

Biblical Citation

A voice came from the throne saying, "Praise our God all you who serve him, you who revere him, small and great!" Then I heard something like the roar of a huge crowd, not unlike the sound of a rushing waterfall or mighty peals of thunder, which cried out: "Alleluia! The Lord, our God, the almighty has taken possession of his kingdom. Let us rejoice and be glad and give him glory, because the day of the wedding feast of the Lamb has arrived. His bride is ready and has been given a garment of splendid linen to wear." (Rv 19:5-8)

Prayer Intentions

- That hope might transform the life of every Christian.
- That all those in authority might work for a future full of peace.

Our Father...

Hail Mary, full of grace, the Lord is with you. Blessed are you among women, and blessed is the fruit of your womb, JESUS...

1 ... who crowned you with goodness, power and glory.
2 ... who has brought you into the power of his kingdom.
3 ... who has made you Queen of the universe.
4 ... who has proclaimed you Mother of all Christians.
5 ... who has entrusted you with the distribution of his graces.
6 ... who has made you Mediatrix and advocate of our race.
7 ... who frees the Church from all error through your intercession.
8 ... who, in you, offers hope to sinners.
9 ... who, with you, consoles the afflicted.
10 ... who fills the hearts of the saints with joy on account of you.

Holy Mary, Mother of God, pray for us sinners, now and at the hour of our death. Amen.

Glory be... O my Jesus...

Salve Regina

Hail, holy Queen, Mother of mercy,
Our life, our sweetness and our hope,
To you do we cry, poor banished children of Eve;
To you do we sigh, mourning and weeping in this valley of tears.
Turn, then, most gracious advocate,
Your eyes of mercy toward us.
And after this, our exile,
Show unto us the blessed fruit of your womb, Jesus.
O clement, O loving, O sweet virgin Mary.

V.   Pray for us, O holy Mother of God.
R.   That we may be made worthy of the promises of Christ.

Let us pray. Pour forth, we beseech You, O Lord, Your grace into
our hearts, that we to whom the Incarnation of Christ, Your Son,
was made known by the message of an angel — may, by his passion and cross, be brought to the glory of his resurrection, through
the same Christ, our Lord. Amen.

Concluding Prayer

Let us pray. O God, whose only begotten Son, by his life, death
and resurrection, has purchased for us the rewards of eternal life,
grant, we beseech You, that meditating on these mysteries of the
Most Holy Rosary of the Blessed Virgin Mary, we may imitate
what they contain and obtain what they promise through the same
Christ, our Lord. Amen.

Litany of the Blessed Virgin Mary

Lord, have mercy on us.	*Lord, have mercy on us.*
Christ, have mercy on us.	*Christ, have mercy on us.*
Lord, have mercy on us.	*Lord, have mercy on us.*
Christ, hear us.	*Christ, graciously hear us.*
God, the Father of heaven,	*Have mercy on us.*
God, the Son, Redeemer of the world,	*Have mercy on us.*
God, the Holy Spirit,	*Have mercy on us.*
Holy Trinity, one God,	*Have mercy on us.*
Holy Mary,	*Pray for us.*
Holy Mother of God,	*Pray for us.*
Holy Virgin of virgins,	*Pray for us.*
Mother of Christ,	*Pray for us.*
Mother of divine grace,	*Pray for us.*
Mother most pure,	*Pray for us.*
Mother most chaste,	*Pray for us.*
Mother inviolate,	*Pray for us.*
Mother undefiled,	*Pray for us.*
Mother most amiable,	*Pray for us.*
Mother most admirable,	*Pray for us.*
Mother of good counsel,	*Pray for us.*
Mother of our Creator,	*Pray for us.*
Mother of our Redeemer,	*Pray for us.*
Virgin most prudent,	*Pray for us.*
Virgin most renowned,	*Pray for us.*
Virgin most powerful,	*Pray for us.*
Virgin most merciful,	*Pray for us.*
Virgin most faithful,	*Pray for us.*
Mirror of justice,	*Pray for us.*
Seat of wisdom,	*Pray for us.*
Cause of our joy,	*Pray for us.*
Spiritual vessel,	*Pray for us.*

Vessel of honor,	*Pray for us.*
Vessel of singular devotion,	*Pray for us.*
Mystical rose,	*Pray for us.*
Tower of David,	*Pray for us.*
Tower of ivory,	*Pray for us.*
House of gold,	*Pray for us.*
Ark of the covenant,	*Pray for us.*
Gate of heaven,	*Pray for us.*
Morning star,	*Pray for us.*
Health of the sick,	*Pray for us.*
Refuge of sinners,	*Pray for us.*
Comforter of the afflicted,	*Pray for us.*
Help of Christians,	*Pray for us.*
Queen of Angels,	*Pray for us.*
Queen of Patriarchs,	*Pray for us.*
Queen of Prophets,	*Pray for us.*
Queen of Apostles,	*Pray for us.*
Queen of Martyrs,	*Pray for us.*
Queen of Confessors,	*Pray for us.*
Queen of Virgins,	*Pray for us.*
Queen of all Saints,	*Pray for us.*
Queen conceived without original sin,	*Pray for us.*
Queen assumed into heaven,	*Pray for us.*
Queen of the most holy Rosary,	*Pray for us.*
Queen of peace,	*Pray for us.*

V. Pray for us, O holy Mother of God.

R. That we may be made worthy of the promises of Christ.

Let us pray. Grant Your servants continual health of mind and body, O Lord God. Let the intercession of the blessed ever-virgin Mary gain for us freedom from our present sorrow and bring us to the joy of everlasting happiness, through Christ our Lord. Amen.

About the Frescoes

Giotto was the first European artist to make a lasting mark as painter, sculptor and architect since the days of Greek antiquity. Before him, painting was still considered a craft, a "mechanical" art. In his lifetime, however, Giotto changed all that, and within ten years of his death was called by Boccaccio in his *Decameron* "the greatest painter in the world." In fact, he had raised painting to such a prestigious level among the arts that it influenced sculpture rather than vice versa. Giotto came to occupy a position of great respect not only in Florence, a city that was one of the most important centers of trade in Europe, but the impulse he gave to the arts was so great that it determined the destiny of European painting for several centuries. His rediscovery of the third dimension, of real and measurable space, of the natural appearances of surfaces, of the individualizing aspects of reality became part and parcel of European art for years to come. The frescoes that make up four of the five panels for the Luminous Mysteries are from the Arena Chapel in Padua, Italy (Capella Scrovegni).

Blessed Fra Angelico (1400-1455)

Beatified in 1982 by Pope John Paul II, Blessed Fra Angelico was an Italian painter of the early Renaissance who combined the life of a devout friar with that of an accomplished artist. He was called Angelico (Italian for "angelic") and Beato (Italian for "blessed") because the paintings he did were of calm, religious subjects and because of his extraordinary piety. Guido di Pietro (his baptismal name) grew up in Tuscany and entered a Dominican convent in Fiesole when he was 18. He took the name Giovanni da Fiesole and began his career as an illuminator of missals and other religious books. He gradually graduated from that to doing altarpieces that soon drew the attention of his superiors. In 1436, he was sent to the newly renovated Dominican convent of San Marco in Florence to paint frescoes for the cloister, chapter house, and entrances to the 20 cells on the upper corridors. One of the most impressive of these is *The Transfiguration*, which, in addition to the illustrations from the *Armadio degli Argenti*, is depicted in this booklet. In 1445 he was summoned to Rome by Pope Eugenius IV to paint frescoes for the now destroyed Chapel of the Sacrament in the Vatican, and from 1449 to 1452 he served as prior of the convent in Fiesole. He died in the Dominican convent in Rome on March 18, 1455, and his tomb is in the church of Santa Maria sopra Minerva. His feast day is February 18.